**W9-BRD-190**

# ENERGY Revolution

# Generating Wind Power

## Niki Walker

 Crabtree Publishing Company

![Crabtree logo]

# Crabtree Publishing Company

www.crabtreebooks.com

**Coordinating editor:** Ellen Rodger

**Series editor:** Carrie Gleason

**Project editor:** Adrianna Morganelli

**Editors:** Rachel Eagen, L. Michelle Nielsen

**Production coordinator:** Rosie Gowsell

**Production assistant and layout:** Samara Parent

**Art director:** Rob MacGregor

**Photo research:** Allison Napier

**Photographs:** Paul Glendell/Alamy: p. 13; AP/Wide World Photos: p. 14, p. 17 (top), p. 26 (bottom), p. 28, p. 29; Corbis: p. 3 (bottom left); Macduff Everton/Corbis: p. 19 (top); Peter Johnson/Corbis: p. 22; Layne Kennedy/Corbis: p. 25 (top); John and Lisa Merrill/Corbis: p. 19 (bottom); Bob Sacha/Corbis: p. 24; Ingo Wagner/dpa/Corbis: p. 17 (bottom); Tony West/Corbis: p. 27; Ed Young/Corbis: cover; DOE/NREL-Herald Rutland: p. 20 (top right); Keystone/Getty Images: p. 21 (top); The Granger Collection, New York: p. 20 (bottom left); Betsy Dupuis/istock International: Rosie the Riveter icon; John Beatty/Photo Researchers, Inc.: p. 15 (bottom); Pat Caulfield/Photo Researchers, Inc.: p. 8 (bottom); Other Images from stock CD.

**Cover:** Wind turbines are at work producing electricity at a wind farm in California.

**Title page:** Historians believe the smock mill was invented by the Dutch in the 1500s. Smock mills fell out of use in the 1800s, when wind power began to be replaced by steam power.

**Library and Archives Canada Cataloguing in Publication**

Walker, Niki, 1972-
    Generating wind power / Niki Walker.

(Energy revolution)
Includes index.
ISBN-13: 978-0-7787-2913-6 (bound)
ISBN-10: 0-7787-2913-3 (bound)
ISBN-13: 978-0-7787-2927-3 (pbk)
ISBN-10: 0-7787-2927-3 (pbk)
        1. Wind power--Juvenile literature.  I. Title.  II. Series.

TJ820.W34 2006        j621.4'5        C2006-902466-9

**Library of Congress Cataloging-in-Publication Data**

Walker, Niki, 1972-
    Generating wind power / written by Niki Walker.
        p. cm. -- (Energy revolution)
Includes index.
ISBN-13: 978-0-7787-2913-6 (rlb)
ISBN-10: 0-7787-2913-3 (rlb)
ISBN-13: 978-0-7787-2927-3 (pbk)
ISBN-10: 0-7787-2927-3 (pbk)
    1. Wind power--Juvenile literature.  I. Title.  II. Series.
TJ820.W355 2006
621.4'5--dc22
                                        2006014370

## Crabtree Publishing Company

www.crabtreebooks.com        1-800-387-7650

**Published in Canada**
**Crabtree Publishing**
616 Welland Ave.
St. Catharines, ON
L2M 5V6

**Published in the United States**
**Crabtree Publishing**
PMB16A
350 Fifth Ave., Suite 3308
New York, NY  10118

**Published in the United Kingdom**
**Crabtree Publishing**
White Cross Mills
High Town, Lancaster
LA1 4XS

**Published in Australia**
**Crabtree Publishing**
386 Mt. Alexander Rd.
Ascot Vale (Melbourne)
VIC 3032

# Contents

## Energy Conservation: 'We Can Do It!'

"We Can Do It" was a slogan that appeared on posters made during World War II. One poster featured "Rosie the Riveter," a woman dressed in blue coveralls (shown below). The poster was originally intended to encourage women to enter the workforce in industry to replace the men who left to serve in the war. Today, the image of Rosie the Riveter represents a time when people came together as a society to reach a common goal. Today's energy challenge can be combatted in a similar way. Together, we can work to save our planet from the pollution caused by burning fossil fuels by learning to conserve energy and developing alternative energy sources.

We Can Do It!

WAR PRODUCTION CO-ORDINATING COMMITTEE

# Energy at Work

Energy is all around us. People capture and control the energy in wind to do work, such as pump water, sail boats, and produce electricity. Wind has a type of energy called kinetic energy, or the energy of motion. The faster wind blows, the more energy it has.

## Conservation Tip

Energy conservation means reducing the amount of power that we use. You can find tips on how to conserve energy, and facts about energy conservation in boxes like these.

## What is Energy?

Energy is the capacity to do work or make something happen. Without energy, the world would be dark, cold, silent, and completely still. Energy makes people, animals, and plants live and grow. People use energy to run machines, cook food, and heat buildings. Energy cannot be created or destroyed, but can be transferred, or moved, from one thing to another. For example, a windmill's blades turn when the wind blows against them. This is because the wind's kinetic energy is transferred to the blades.

*(above) Fierce storm winds have a lot of energy. They are strong enough to blow trains from their tracks and rip the roofs off buildings.*

## Changing Energy

Energy can be converted, or changed, from one form to another. Wind energy is converted into electricity by using machines called wind turbines. It is not possible to convert all of wind's energy into electricity. Some of the energy changes into a form that is not useful at the time, such as heat energy. The goal in converting energy is efficiency, or changing as much of it as possible into a useable form.

## Limited vs. Unlimited

Anything that has energy that people can use is an energy source. There are two basic types of energy sources: non-renewable and renewable sources. Non-renewable sources cannot be replaced once they are used. Fossil fuels, such as coal, oil, and natural gas are non-renewable. Renewable sources, which are often called alternative energy sources, are continually replenished by people or nature. Wind is a renewable source, as well as **biomass**, hydro, or running water, and the Sun.

## Electric Power

Power is the rate at which energy is used up doing work. Usually, people refer to "power" when describing electricity. Electricity, or electric power, is measured in watts. The amount of electricity that household appliances use is also measured in watts. The higher an appliance's wattage, the more electricity it uses. Below are some common household appliances and the power they use:

**REFRIGERATOR 500 watts**

**HAIR DRYER 1,250 watts**

**COMPUTER 360 watts**

# Energy Problems

Fossil fuels are the most commonly used energy source in the world, but they are harmful to the environment and people's health. People worry about what will happen when we use up our supply of fossil fuels. For these reasons, people are becoming more interested in alternative energy sources, such as the wind.

*(background) Oil is transported around the world by ships, trucks, and pipelines. Sometimes, accidents occur and the oil spills or leaks into the oceans and onto land. This pollutes the water and kills wildlife and plants.*

## Hurting the Environment

Burning fossil fuels releases harmful gases into the air, which creates pollution. The gas sulfur dioxide is a product of burning fossil fuels. When sulfur dioxide rises into the air and mixes with the water in clouds, it forms acid rain, which damages forests and buildings and poisons wildlife when it falls. Greenhouse gases, such as carbon dioxide, are also released into the air when fossil fuels are burned. Greenhouse gases trap the Sun's heat in the **atmosphere**. This results in global warming, or a gradual rise in Earth's temperatures. Many scientists believe that if global warming continues, other problems will result, such as severe storms, floods, droughts, and the loss of habitat of many plants and animals.

## A Limited Supply

Scientists are not sure exactly when fossil fuels will run out. Some estimate that there is enough oil left to last about 40 years, enough natural gas to last about 70 years, and enough coal to last about 250 years. As our supply of fossil fuels shrinks, the price to buy them will rise. Most of the technology used every day depends on fossil fuels to run. Cars run on gasoline, furnaces need coal, oil, or natural gas, and most power plants use fossil fuels to produce electricity. In order to keep today's technology running, other energy sources are needed.

*(above) Burning fossil fuels creates smog. Smog is a form of air pollution that makes breathing difficult and harms people's health.*

# Energy Dependence

Oil is found in certain areas of the world, and few countries have their own supply. Many countries buy oil from the Middle East, where most of the world's oil is found. If the price to purchase oil is high, the cost for people to use it also rises. This means that driving cars and heating homes becomes expensive. To ensure a steady, affordable energy supply, countries need to use more of the energy sources that they already have, such as the wind.

*High oil costs make it expensive to fuel vehicles.*

# Air on the Move

Wind is created when warm air, heated by the Sun, rises, and cold air sweeps in to take its place. The wind blows all over the planet, but coastal and mountainous areas have more steady and reliable winds than other areas.

## Mountains and Valleys

Mountainous areas have predictable wind patterns. During the day, the warm air above a mountain slope blows toward the mountain's top. This creates what is called a valley wind. At night, when the air cools, the wind blows down toward the valley, forming a mountain wind. Mountain winds are also called katabatic winds. When katabatic winds blow into narrow valleys between mountains, their speed increases. This is known as the tunnel effect. Katabatic winds are called special names in different areas of the world, such as the Chinook in the Rocky Mountains, and the Santa Ana in California.

*(above) The strongest winds blow across Antarctica. In winter, the winds reach speeds of more than 100 miles per hour (160 kilometers per hour).*

*(below) Winds are greatly affected by the land and water over which they blow. They can be slowed down by rough surfaces and obstacles, such as forests and tall buildings. Winds blow steadily across wide open areas such as plains and deserts.*

# Land and Sea Breezes

Water does not heat up as quickly as land does, so the air above a body of water is cooler than air over land. During the day, warm air above land rises, and cooler air from above water sweeps in to take its place. This wind is known as a sea breeze. At night, the wind changes direction because land cools faster than water does, so the air above the water is warmer. The warm air above the water rises, and the cool air above land sweeps in to take its place. This wind is called a land breeze. Land breezes are generally weaker than sea breezes. This is why coastal areas are windy.

## Conservation Tip

Only a small amount of energy that a light bulb uses is turned into light. The rest is wasted, and is turned into heat. To save energy, turn off lights when they are not needed, and use compact fluorescent bulbs.

## Seasonal Differences

Seasons also affect the speed and strength of winds. In most areas of North America, winds are usually strongest in winter and spring when there are many storms. In California, the strongest winds often occur during the summer. This is because the winds are affected by the differences in temperature between the Pacific Ocean, the mountains, and the Mojave Desert, which lies to the east of the mountains.

# Wind Turbines

Wind is harnessed and converted into electricity using machines called wind turbines. The amount of electricity that a turbine produces depends on its size and the speed of the wind.

## How Wind Turbines Work

All wind turbines have the same basic parts: blades, a tower, and a gearbox. These parts work together to capture the wind's kinetic energy and convert it into electricity.

1. The wind blows against the blades and makes them turn.
2. The blades are connected to a main shaft, or pole. As the blades turn, the main shaft turns.
3. The main shaft is connected to a gearbox. Inside the gearbox, large gears slowly turn, which makes smaller gears turn quickly.
4. The gears turn another shaft, called the high-speed shaft, very quickly.
5. The high-speed shaft is connected to a generator, which is made up of magnets inside coils of copper wire. When the high-speed shaft spins, the magnets spin, which creates an electric current in the wire.
6. Thick cables carry the electric current, or electricity, out of the turbine.

## Horizontal Axis Turbines

The most common type of wind turbine is the horizontal axis turbine. It has two or three blades that spin around a horizontal shaft. The blades are joined in the center by a hub. Together, the blades and the hub are called the rotor. The rotor is mounted on top of a tall tower, where the wind blows freely without obstacles to slow it down. The rotor is attached to a compartment called the nacelle, which contains the gearbox, the generator, and a computer. The computer tracks the wind's speed and direction. When the wind's direction changes, the computer activates a motor to turn the nacelle, which moves the rotor into the wind. The rotor will only spin when it is facing into the wind.

*(above) The rotors of horizontal axis turbines are mounted high above the ground on top of tall towers, where the wind is not slowed by obstacles, such as hills and trees.*

### Conservation Tip

By conserving hot water, you are saving both water and the energy used to heat it. Use hot water wisely when you bathe or shower, and wash your hands, clothes, and dishes.

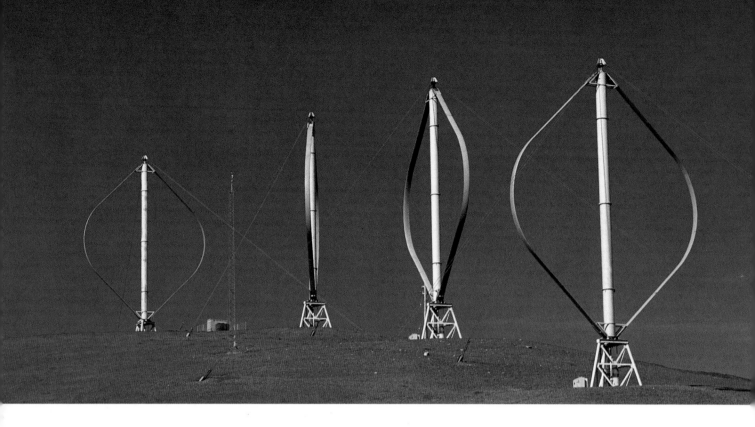

## Vertical Axis Turbines

Vertical axis turbines have two or three blades that spin around a vertical, or upright, shaft. The turbines do not need computers to move them into the wind, because the blades catch the wind from any direction. The gearbox is located near the ground at the base of the tower, which is thin and light. Vertical axis turbines produce less electricity than horizontal axis turbines because their blades are closer to the ground where the wind is slowed down by obstacles, such as trees.

## Conservation Tip

Batteries contain a dangerous metal called mercury, which leaks into the ground when they are thrown away. Try to use devices powered by alternative energies, such as calculators that run on solar energy.

## Size and Power

Wind turbines come in different sizes. Small turbines have rotors from three to 50 feet (one to 15 m) in **diameter**. Their towers reach up to 130 feet (40 m) high. They can generate up to 20 **kilowatts** (kW) of electricity and are used to power homes, farm equipment, and small villages. Large turbines are often called utility-scale turbines because they generate enough power for utilities, or electricity companies, to sell. Early utility-scale turbines that generate between 50 and 100 kilowatts of electricity are being replaced with larger turbines that generate thousands of kilowatts. The largest turbines generate up to five **megawatts** (MW) of electricity, which is enough energy to power 5,000 homes! Today, the rotors and towers of utility-scale turbines range from 164 feet (50 m) to 295 feet (90 m) in length.

*(above) Vertical axis turbines operate in the air flow near the ground.*

## Safety Measures

The faster the wind blows, the faster a wind turbine's blades spin. Strong winds can make the blades spin so fast that the turbine vibrates, which can damage the blades, or cause them to snap off. To prevent these accidents, turbines are designed to reach a maximum speed, which varies according to the turbine's size. When a utility-scale turbine reaches its maximum speed, its computer tilts the blades to catch less wind to slow them. This is called furling. Computers also activate brakes on the rotor to slow the blades. The rotors of most small turbines are attached to the towers on a hinge. When the turbine reaches its maximum speed, the rotor tilts on the hinges out of the wind to slow the blades down.

*A maintenance worker checks the condition of this wind turbine's blades at a wind farm in England.*

# Wind Farms

Wind farms, also called wind power plants, are made up of several wind turbines grouped together to produce large amounts of electricity.

## Siting

Choosing a location for a wind farm is called siting. It is very important that the site has strong, steady winds. Developers, or the people building a wind farm, study and measure the wind of an area before building a wind farm there. The best sites for wind farms are the coasts of large lakes and oceans, hilltops, open plains, and mountain passes. Developers must determine whether or not it is possible to connect to the **power grid** from the site. What impact the wind farm will have on wildlife is also considered. They need to get permission from the community or government before the wind farm can be built.

## Arranging Turbines

Once a site for a wind farm is chosen, developers plan the placement of the wind turbines. The turbines are usually arranged in rows facing in the direction of the **prevailing wind**. Wind turbines are usually spaced about five to nine times the diameter of their rotors apart. Turbines with rotors 165 feet (50 meters) across are spaced 825 to 1,485 feet (251 to 453 meters) apart. If turbines are placed too close together, they block one another's wind. Placing the turbines too far apart wastes space on the wind farm.

*Supporters of a plan to put wind turbines off the coast of Cape Cod, Massachusetts, meet with government and environmental leaders to discuss the benefits of the project.*

(above) Wind farms located on hillsides take up less space than those on flat plains. On hillsides, turbines are arranged on a slope, and are not positioned directly in front of one another.

(below) Wind speed is measured with a device called an anemometer. Most anemometers have three arms with cups at the end to catch the wind. The wind pushes against the arms and makes them spin. The harder the wind blows, the faster they spin.

## From Farm to Grid

The electricity that wind farms generate is sent to the power grid, which delivers electricity to homes, schools, factories, and other buildings. The electricity flows along cables from the wind farm to a network of underground wires, which lead to a substation. The substation has a transformer, which is a device that increases the electricity to a very high voltage, or force. High-voltage electricity travels more efficiently along power lines, so less electricity gets lost along the way. The high-voltage electricity flows from the substation to power lines throughout the grid.

Substations and transformers at the other end of the power lines transform the electricity to lower voltages before it flows into homes and other buildings. The voltage must be lowered so that appliances and other electric devices can run on it safely.

## Harvesting Wind

In many parts of North America, farmers and ranchers are increasing their earnings by farming the wind. Developers build wind farms on farmland, and pay the farmers and ranchers **rent** or a share of the wind farm's earnings. The turbines do not interfere with ranching or farming. Cattle and sheep graze under the turbines, and farmers can plant crops right up close to the base of each turbine.

*(above) Cattle graze beneath wind turbines at a wind farm.*

CASE STUDY

# Powering Schools

In 1993, Spirit Lake Elementary School, in Spirit Lake, Iowa, became the first school in the United States to be powered by wind. The school's electricity is produced by a 250 kW wind turbine located behind the playground. In 2001, a second turbine was built to power Spirit Lake's middle school, high school, bus shelter, and football stadium. This turbine sends electricity directly to the power grid. The utility keeps track of how much electricity the turbine sends to the power grid and how much electricity the schools use from the grid. If the turbine produces more electricity than the schools use, the utility pays the schools for the electricity.

SCHOOL BUS

# Offshore Wind Farms

Offshore wind farms are located in the shallow waters of coastlines. There are several reasons for putting wind turbines offshore. Many small European countries, such as Denmark, Sweden, and Holland, are running out of space for wind farms on land. Winds blow stronger and more steadily across water than they do over land, because they encounter fewer obstacles. This means there is more energy offshore for turbines to harness. Offshore turbines produce about 50 percent more electricity than turbines on land. Underwater construction for offshore wind farms is difficult and expensive. The bottoms of the towers and the cables that carry electricity from the turbines must be buried deep into the seabed. It is also more difficult to maintain and repair offshore turbines.

*(above) The Jersey-Atlantic wind farm, off the coast of Atlantic City, in New Jersey, is the United States' first offshore wind farm. It began operating in December 2005. The offshore farm is made up of five turbines that each produce 1.5 megawatts of electricity.*

*(right) Offshore wind turbines are not as tall as turbines on land. This is because there are few obstacles over water to slow down the wind.*

# Wind Power History

People have been harnessing the wind's power for thousands of years. Some of the first machines invented ran on wind power. Ancient peoples found ways to use the wind's energy to do work, which made their lives easier.

## Blowing Down the Nile

Many historians believe that the first machine to use wind power was the sailboat. The first known sails were used by ancient Egyptians around 3200 B.C. to sail along the Nile River, in Egypt. The Egyptians used the boats for travel and to transport **cargo** to parts of the country. The sails were square and made of woven reeds or leaves. Square sails allowed people to sail easily in the direction the wind was blowing. It was difficult to sail in other directions because the sails could not be turned on their **masts** to catch the wind.

## Setting Sail

During the 800s, **Arab** sailors invented a triangular sail called the lateen sail. The lateen sail could be turned on its mast to catch the wind from almost any direction. Unlike square sails, the lateen sail worked even if the wind was not blowing behind it. Boats equipped with lateen sails were easier to steer. By the 1400s, European explorers were sailing in ships equipped with lateen sails.

*Today, modern sailboats use lateen sails.*

## Early Windmills

The first windmills were used in Persia, which is present-day Iran, around 700 A.D. People used windmills to grind grain and to pump water to drink, for their livestock, and to water, or **irrigate**, their crops. The windmills were made up of an upright shaft that had sails attached to it. The sails were made of cloth or palm leaves. As the sails caught the wind, they turned the shaft, which operated a water pump or rolled a heavy stone over grains to grind them.

## European Windmills

Europeans began building windmills during the 1100s. Historians believe that European soldiers had seen windmills while fighting the **Crusades** in the Middle East, and returned home with stories about them. Until then, Europeans had relied on water wheels to power mills to grind grain and saw wood. Water wheels could only be used in rivers and streams, which often froze in winter. Windmills soon became popular in Europe because wind power was available year-round and they could be built anywhere there was wind.

*(right) The tower mill was developed in France in the 1600s. The mill's tower was made of brick or stone, and housed the miller's family, grinding equipment, grains, and flour. The sails were attached to a cap that could be rotated around the top of the tower to turn the sails into the wind.*

*(above) A type of windmill called a post mill was built in Holland in the mid-1200s. The windmill was mounted on a post. When the wind changed direction, the miller, or mill operator, rotated the entire mill on the post until the sails faced the wind.*

## Windmills and the West

In the mid-1800s, thousands of people across western North America owned windmills. North American windmills were small and had towers built of wooden beams and narrow wooden blades. Farmers and ranchers used the windmills to pump water from underground to irrigate their land. The wooden blades were replaced with blades made of steel in 1870. Steel blades were much more efficient because they could be curved and shaped to catch more wind. Windmills became more popular across the West in the late 1800s. Electric lights and appliances became available, but there were no power lines in the West to bring people electricity. People connected their windmills to generators to produce small amounts of electricity to power lights and charge batteries.

*(left) Daniel Halladay developed the first North American windmill in 1854. It turned itself into the wind and controlled its own speed.*

## Wind Power in Vermont

In 1941, the world's first utility-scale turbine was built on a mountaintop in Vermont, U.S.A. The turbine was 110 feet (33 meters) tall and its blades were 75 feet (23 meters) long. It produced 1.25 MW of electricity. The turbine worked for four years, until one of its blades broke off. The turbine was torn down in 1946.

## Blowing off Wind Power

Wind power became less popular in the 1930s and 1940s. The demand for electricity grew as more electric household appliances became available. Small windmills and generators could not supply enough electricity to regularly power these appliances. The Canadian and U.S. governments installed power lines throughout the West, which added to the decline of wind power. After **World War II** ended in 1945, the price of fossil fuels dropped, and electricity from power plants became less expensive. Wind power could not compete with the new power grid, and windmills fell out of use.

## The 1973 Oil Crisis

In 1973, a group of oil-producing countries in the Middle East refused to sell oil to European countries and the United States. They also reduced the amount of oil they sold to other countries around the world. Europeans and North Americans faced an energy crisis. The demand for oil was far greater than how much oil was available, which caused the costs of driving vehicles and heating homes to soar. When the oil crisis ended in 1974, oil was four times the price it was in 1973.

### Conservation Tip

Many vehicles use fossil fuels as their energy source. When vehicles burn fossil fuels, gases that pollute the air are produced. Help save energy and the Earth by taking the bus, riding a bicycle, or walking.

## Wind Power Picks Up

After the oil crisis, many governments reduced their countries' dependence on oil, encouraging people to use alternative energy sources. Throughout the 1970s and 1980s, countries in Europe and North America developed large wind turbines. The turbines were built from lighter and sturdier materials, and had two or three long blades. They were more efficient, and could deliver more wind-powered electricity to homes and buildings. In the early 1980s, wind farms were built in California, Denmark, and Germany. Many North Americans lost interest in renewable energy sources when the price of fossil fuels dropped in the mid-1980s. Throughout the 1990s, designers continued improving wind turbines, and wind power grew in European countries, including Denmark and Germany.

*(above) Four men ride horses in Amsterdam, in the Netherlands, during the 1973 oil crisis on a day when driving vehicles was prohibited.*

# Wind at Work

The use of wind power is on the rise in the United States, Canada, Denmark, Germany, the United Kingdom, and many other countries. Today, wind power is the fastest-growing source of electricity in the world. In addition to electricity, wind energy is also used for many other jobs.

## Today's Windmills

There are about one million windmills at work around the world today. Windmills that are used to pump water from underground are called windpumps. This water is used for drinking, cooking, watering crops, and raising livestock. Some windmills are still used to grind grain into flour.

## Improving Lives

Wind power is helping to improve people's lives in dry, hot countries where water is scarce, such as some African countries. Windpumps draw water from underground and pump it into storage tanks. People use the water for drinking, washing, and farming. Villagers often do not have access to a power grid, and cannot afford to purchase fossil fuels to power generators. Small wind turbines are used to run generators that create enough electricity to power lights, televisions, and radios. The wind turbines are part of a hybrid, or mixed, system, which produces electricity by using wind and solar energy. The hybrid system provides villagers with reliable power that they can afford.

*An elephant drinks from a water source that was created by pumping water from underground with a windpump.*

## Small Turbines

Today, thousands of people in the United States, Canada, and Europe use small turbines to supply electricity to their homes or businesses. Their buildings are also connected to the power grid. When the wind is not blowing or extra electricity is needed, they take electricity from the power grid. Any extra electricity the turbine produces goes into the power grid. Utilities pay the turbine owners for this electricity or provide them with the same amount of electricity for free when it is needed. This practice is called net metering.

*(below) Windpumps in Morocco, in Africa, pump water into storage tanks, which supply homes and communities with clean water.*

**CASE STUDY**

# Water for Morocco

The country of Morocco in northern Africa is very hot and dry. People in many villages have difficulty getting drinking water because there are few rivers and streams. They must pump water from underground sources and move it to storage tanks. In the past, Moroccans relied on pumps powered by diesel fuel, which is made from oil. In some villages, people could not run their pumps because they could not afford to purchase the fuel. In other villages, people had enough diesel fuel to work their pumps for only a few hours each day. Since the 1980s, Morocco's diesel pumps have begun to be replaced with windpumps. These pumps run for free, and pump water into storage tanks as long as the wind blows. In some villages, people have three times more drinking water than they did in the past.

# The Drawbacks

Like all energy sources, wind power has many benefits, but it also has many drawbacks. Wind is not available all the time, wind turbines are expensive to build, and delivering power from the windiest places to cities and towns where it is needed can be difficult. Wind turbines can disturb natural **habitats** and harm wildlife. Many people feel that wind turbines are unattractive, and argue that they are noisy.

## The Perks

**Wind energy does not have the same negative effects that fossil fuels do. Wind energy does not release carbon dioxide, sulphur dioxide, or any other air pollution. It does not produce dangerous wastes. The wind is a free, renewable source of energy that is available everywhere on Earth.**

## Intermittent Power

Wind power is only available when the wind blows, but utilities must be able to supply people's demand for electricity all the time. Back-up power plants supply electricity when the wind is not blowing. Power plant operators must carefully time the switch between plants to avoid disrupting the flow of electricity to their customers. Home owners who rely on the wind to power their appliances also need a back-up for calm days. Batteries can store the wind's energy, but they usually store enough power to last only a few days. The largest batteries available are not big enough to store power for utilities.

*If the wind does not blow hard enough, turbines cannot produce electricity. Utility-scale turbines need winds to blow at least 12 miles per hour (19 kilometers per hour) to work.*

## The Cost

To attract customers, an energy source has to cost about the same amount as fossil fuels. Electricity from wind farms is much less expensive today than it was in the 1970s, but in many areas it still costs more than electricity from coal or natural gas-powered plants. As wind turbines become more efficient, the cost of producing electricity from wind will decline. Today, it costs millions of dollars to build a wind farm. Small turbines for homes cost several thousand dollars. Although owners of small turbines use them to generate free energy, they must be willing to spend a lot of money initially to do so.

*(above) The amount of energy it takes to make, install, and operate a wind turbine is usually earned back within months of operating the turbine.*

## Long-Distance Delivery

The United States and Canada have enough wind to generate all the electricity they need, but the windiest sites are far from the areas that need electricity and often from a power grid. Even in areas where power lines exist, many of the lines are old and too small to carry extra electricity generated from a wind farm. To deliver the electricity, new power lines need to be built.

## Conservation Tip

Almost half of the energy used in homes is for heat. You can reduce the amount of fossil fuels being used for heating by dressing warmly indoors, and keeping the heat as low as you comfortably can.

## Environmental Impacts

Many of the best sites for wind farms are in wilderness areas, but building wind farms affects these natural environments. In some cases, trees are cleared so that they do not block the wind. The cement bases on which turbines rest must be set deep into the ground. The holes for the bases are often blasted using **dynamite**, which frightens or injures animals. Turbines are transported to the site by heavy trucks, which requires roads to be built. The trucks disturb wildlife and pollute the air. Power lines are also installed to carry electricity from the wind farm to the power grid.

*(below) Workers pour the cement foundation for a wind turbine in Judith Gap, Montana.*

## Affecting Wildlife

Each year, thousands of birds and bats are killed by flying into the blades of wind turbines. Most of the deaths occur at wind farms that were built in the 1980s, and fewer deaths occur at new wind farms. Many scientists believe this is due to the types of turbines at old wind farms. Older turbines' blades spin much faster and lower to the ground than new turbines. The blades are at a height at which birds and bats fly. The blades of new turbines are higher and spin slower. Scientists have also found that the sites of many old wind farms are located in areas where animals hunt or **migrate**.

*(left and above) More birds and bats are killed each year by house cats, pesticides, and crashing into windows and power lines than are killed by wind turbines.*

## Noise Complaints

Many people argue that wind turbines are noisy. Early wind turbines from the 1970s and 1980s were louder than today's turbines. They were designed so that the wind hit their towers before hitting their rotors. This increased the noise of the wind passing over the blades. Today's turbines face into the wind, so they are much quieter. Placing them a far distance from homes also reduces noise complaints. Most turbines are placed at least 1,640 feet (500 meters) from homes, which makes their noise level about the same as the humming of a refrigerator. Wind turbines may also produce subsonic noise pollution, or sounds that humans cannot hear. Subsonic noises can be felt and heard by animals, which can disrupt their habitats.

## Eye of the Beholder

Some people object to having wind farms built near their homes or scenic areas. They argue that wind turbines spoil the view and may lower the value of their property. In many areas, wind farms have actually increased the value of nearby homes and farms. Wind farms are also tourist attractions. Siting wind farms offshore where turbines are less noticeable can help reduce people's objections to their appearance. Allowing members of a community to help plan and own wind farms can also help.

*(right) A sign protesting wind turbines is nailed to a tree.*

# Making the Change

Wind energy alone cannot replace fossil fuels. In the future, the world's energy needs will be met by a number of energy sources, including the wind. Making the switch from fossil fuels to other energy sources will require planning, time, money, and new attitudes about energy and energy use.

*In many countries, customers choose to buy some of their electricity from wind farms, even when it costs more than other sources. These customers help support and encourage the growth of wind power. In Germany, Europe's largest wind farm generates enough electricity to supply power to more than 30,000 homes.*

## More Wind in the Mix

Electricity from wind power makes up a small part of the electricity North Americans use. To increase the use of wind's energy, several things must happen. Power grids need to be built to connect towns and cities with the windiest sites, which are usually in remote areas. Power lines that are too old or small to carry electricity from wind farms need to be replaced with new lines. Governments must have long-term plans to develop wind power, such as paying some of the cost of building wind farms and installing turbines, requiring utilities to buy specific amounts of wind power, and offering a guarantee to wind farm owners for a certain price for their electricity.

## Working on the Future

One of the best ways to get people to use wind energy is to make it inexpensive. For that to happen, wind turbines need to become more efficient than they are today. The more electricity a turbine produces, the less expensive the electricity becomes. **Engineers** are working on improving designs for larger turbines, which would generate more electricity. They are also trying to make turbines easier and less expensive to build. Experts are working on ways to **forecast** when, where, and how hard the wind will blow. These forecasts will make it easier for utilities to switch between wind farms and other power plants without interrupting the flow of electricity to their customers.

*A developer studies a wind map that shows that Rolette County in North Dakota is a great area for harnessing wind energy.*

## Denmark's Shift to Wind

Denmark is one of the world's leaders in using wind power. About 20 percent of Denmark's electricity is produced from wind energy. Denmark began using wind power in the 1970s. The government wanted to end the country's dependence on oil, so it created a long-term plan to develop wind power. The government offered tax benefits to people who installed wind turbines on their properties. As a result, there are thousands of wind turbines across Denmark today. Almost all of the wind turbines in Denmark are owned by individuals or by cooperatives. Denmark aims to produce 50 percent of its electricity from wind by 2050.

# Timeline

People rely mainly on fossil fuels for energy today, but this has not always been the case. For millions of years, people relied on themselves, animals, moving water, or the wind as energy sources for most work. Alternative energy sources, such as wind energy, have played an important role in human history, and they will become an important part of our future.

*This windpump is used to pump water from underground.*

### 3200 B.C.

Ancient Egyptians invent and use the first boat powered by a sail.

### 700 A.D.

Windmills are used in present-day Iran to pump water and grind grain.

### 1100s

Europeans start to build windmills.

### 1300s

Improvements are made to windmill sails in Europe, which improve windmills' efficiency.

### 1800s

European settlers begin building windmills in North America.

### 1854

Daniel Halladay builds and sells the Halladay Windmill, which is the first windmill designed especially for the West. It has thin wooden blades and turns itself into the wind.

### 1888

Charles F. Brush builds the first large windmill to generate electricity in Cleveland, Ohio.

## 1891

Danish inventor Poul La Cour discovers that fast-turning rotors with few blades generate more electricity than slow-turning rotors with many blades.

## 1920s

G. J. M. Darrieus, a French inventor, designs the first vertical axis wind turbine.

## 1941

The first large-scale turbine in the United States begins operating in Vermont. It supplies electricity until 1945.

## 1971

The first offshore wind farm operates off Denmark's coast.

## 1973

The oil crisis in the United States and other countries sparks new interest in alternative energy, such as solar, wind, and nuclear power.

## 1980s

The first wind farms are built in California, and in Denmark, Germany, and other European countries.

## 1984

The largest vertical axis turbine, Project École, is built in Quebec, Canada. It is 360 feet (110 meters) high.

## 1994

Cowley Ridge, in Alberta, becomes the first utility-grade wind farm in Canada.

## 2003

North Hoyle, the largest offshore wind farm in the United Kingdom, is built.

*(above) A row of horizontal axis turbines at work.*

*(below) Historians believe the Dutch invented the smock mill in the late 1500s. The smock mill consists of a wooden tower, usually with six or eight sides. It has a roof on top that rotates to bring the sails into the wind.*

# Glossary

**Arab** A person from the Middle East or North Africa who speaks the Arabic language

**atmosphere** The layers of gases surrounding Earth

**biomass** Organisms, such as plants, vegetation, and agricultural waste, that are used as an energy source or as a fuel

**cargo** The goods and supplies carried on a ship

**cooperative** An organization owned by all the members, and in which all members profit from the group's work

**Crusades** A series of wars fought from the 1000s to the 1200s in which European Christians tried to claim Palestine and Jerusalem for the Christian Church

**diameter** The length of a straight line that divides a circle into equal halves

**dynamite** A powerful explosive

**engineer** A person who designs bridges, buildings, and other structures

**forecast** To predict, estimate, or calculate in advance

**generator** A machine that converts mechanical energy into electric energy

**habitat** The natural home of an animal or plant

**irrigate** To supply water to crops through ditches, channels, and canals

**kilowatt** A unit of electric power. One kilowatt is equal to 1,000 watts

**mast** A tall pole that supports the sails of a ship

**megawatt** A unit of electric power. One megawatt is equal to one million watts

**Middle East** The countries of Southwest Asia and North Africa

**migrate** To move from one region to another

**pesticide** A chemical used to kill harmful insects

**pipeline** A series of pipes used to carry substances, such as oil, over long distances

**power grid** The system of power lines, generators, and other equipment that brings electricity to homes and other buildings

**prevailing wind** The speed and direction of wind over a particular area on Earth's surface

**rent** Payment made from tenants to landowners for the use of land

**tax** Money collected from people by a government

**World War II** An international war fought mostly in Europe and Asia from 1939 to 1945

# Index

**Printed in the U.S.A.**